THE BALTIMORE BASILICA
AMERICA'S FIRST CATHEDRAL

CELEBRATING 200 YEARS OF RELIGIOUS FREEDOM

MARY-CABRINI DURKIN

THE BASILICA OF THE NATIONAL SHRINE
OF THE ASSUMPTION OF THE BLESSED VIRGIN MARY

BALTIMORE, MARYLAND

The Basilica Historic Trust is a private, nonprofit organization founded in 1976 to maintain, preserve, protect, repair and restore the structure and site of the Baltimore Basilica, together with its grounds and ancillary buildings. The objective is to ensure that the historic and landmark character are preserved for the benefit of future generations of Americans and to foster and promote public knowledge of and interest in the historic nature of the Baltimore Basilica, America's first Cathedral.

PUBLISHER:
Éditions du Signe - B.P. 94
F-67038 Strasbourg Cedex 2
France
Tel 011 333 88 78 91 91
Fax 011 333 88 78 91 99

PUBLISHING DIRECTOR
Christian Riehl

DIRECTOR OF
PUBLICATIONS
Joelle Bernhard

TEXT
Mary Cabrini Durkin

LAYOUT
OM Design

PHOTO ENGRAVING
Atelier du Signe 107229

Printed in China by Sung Fung

© Éditions du Signe, 2006
ISBN 10: 2-7468-1740-3
ISBN 13: 978 -2-7468-1740-1

The book you hold tells the story of the nation's first cathedral and its bicentennial restoration: the rich history and continuing mission of the Basilica of the Assumption.

Maryland was the first place in the English-speaking world with religious freedom, beginning in 1634. The Basilica was built to celebrate the recovery of that freedom in the War for Independence.

Here you will discover how our campaign to "restore the light" has reaffirmed the vision of Archbishop John Carroll and architect Benjamin Henry Latrobe. In stone and in light they celebrated the religious freedom that was essential to the new democratic republic. Their ideal endures, as vital today as two hundred years ago. Since Archbishop Carroll laid its cornerstone in 1806, the Basilica has been at the center of Catholicism in America. It serves the local Baltimore community, the nation, and the world.

As you turn these pages, may you experience the light that fills the Basilica of the Assumption!

Cardinal William H. Keeler
Archbishop of Baltimore

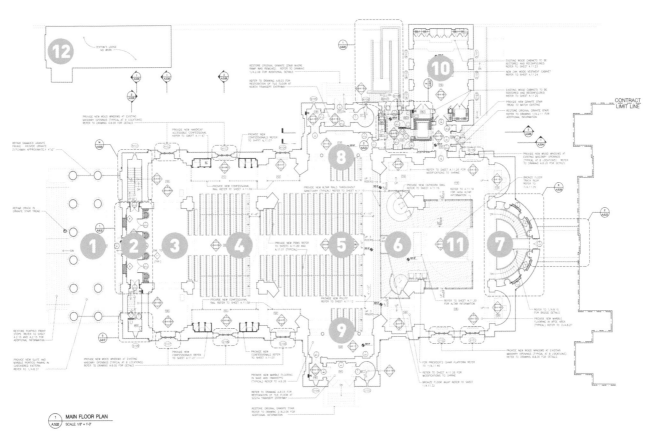

MAIN FLOOR PLAN
SCALE 1/8" = 1'-0"

Reprinted by permission of John G. Waite Associates, Architects PLLC

1. Portico

2. Narthex (West gallery above)

3. West ambulatory

4. Nave

5. Rotunda

6. Sanctuary

7. Apse

8. North transept (Organ loft above)

9. South transept

10. Sacristy

11. Stairs to undercroft

12. Sexton's Lodge (Gift Shop)

TABLE OF CONTENTS

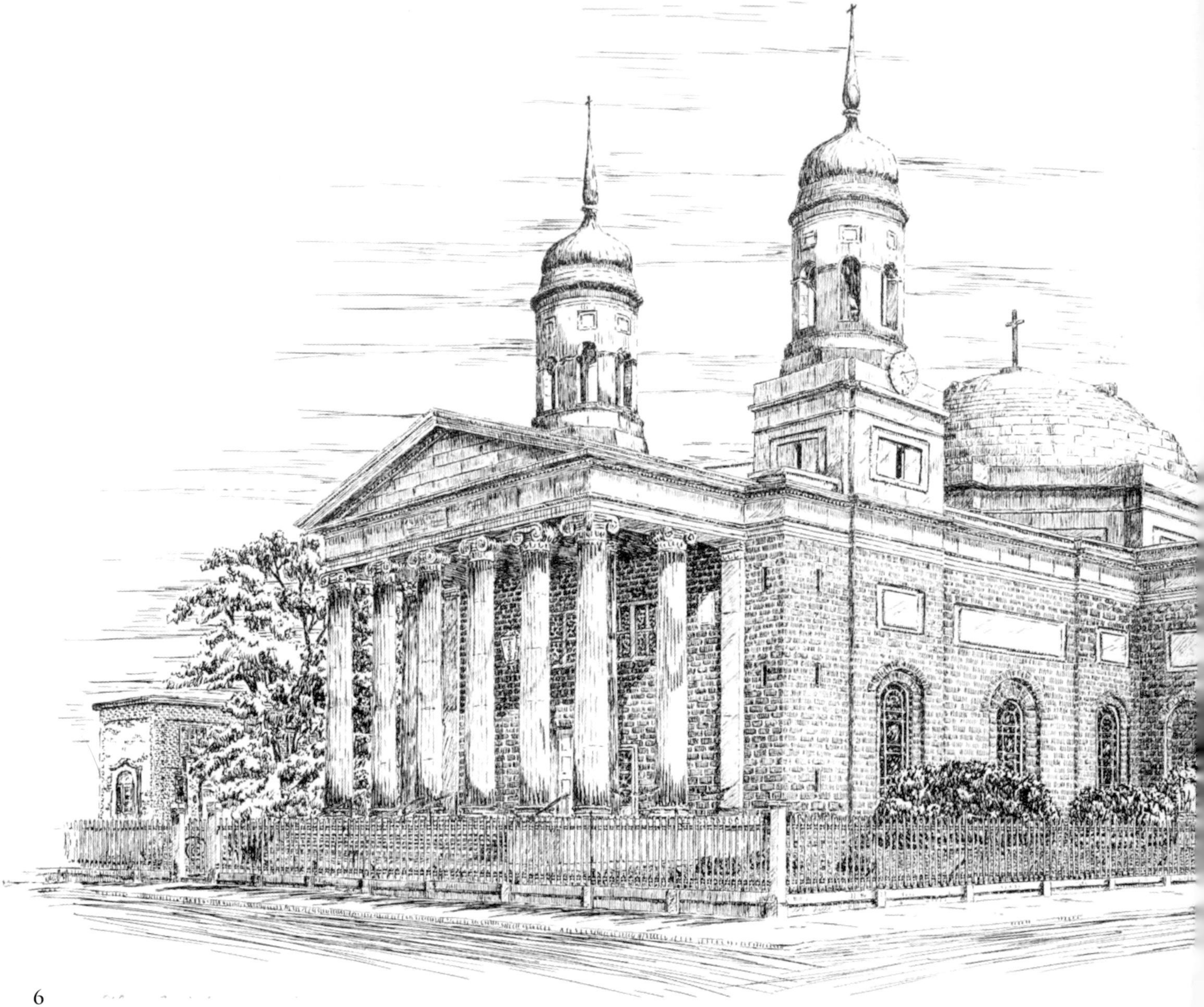

CRADLE OF RELIGIOUS FREEDOM

 When Bishop John Carroll undertook to build the first Catholic cathedral in the United States of America, he recognized the historic significance of this edifice. As the Capitol building stood for the new nation's experiment in democracy, this cathedral would symbolize its experiment in religious freedom.

The ink was barely dry on the Constitution, with its First Amendment guarantee that "Congress shall make no law respecting an establishment of religion, or prohibiting the free exercise thereof...." Only recently an oppressed minority, the Catholic community would emerge from outright persecution to create a shining beacon of liberty.

Baltimore's cathedral would be a symbol, yes, but also a living house of worship. It would be a cradle of American religious freedom.

Etching by Martin Barry provided by the Basilica Historical Trust, Inc.

MOTHER CHURCH OF CATHOLICISM IN AMERICA

E Even John Carroll could not have imagined that two centuries later his cathedral would be the mother church of 60,000,000 Catholics. The events that unfolded within its walls have shaped this vast faith community.

THE LOUISIANA PURCHASE UNDER THE JURISDICTION OF THE ARCHBISHOP OF BALTIMORE 1803 - 1815

THE DIOCESE OF BALTIMORE 1789 - 1810

The Diocese of Baltimore grew as the United States expanded. (Photo courtesy of the Basilica of the Assumption Historic Trust, Inc.)

As the United States of America came to birth, Catholics welcomed independence from Britain. Many served in the revolutionary army. The most distinguished of their number, Charles Carroll of Carrollton, was a signatory to the Declaration of Independence in 1776. His cousin John Carroll later wrote, "In 1776.... Catholics were placed on a level with their fellow-Christians."

When the new nation's Constitution was hammered out in 1789, Catholics breathed deeply and rejoiced. According to the Bill of Rights, United States citizens would face no religious test, support no established church, suffer no discrimination along religious lines. Daniel Carroll, the future bishop's brother, was among the Constitution's signers.

There were between 25,000 and 30,000 Catholics in the country by John Carroll's estimate in 1785, 15,800 of them in Maryland. The nation was a mission field, still being planted and still under the jurisdiction of the Vicar Apostolic of the London District, England. But it was time for the Church to take root in these new United States.

Archbishop John Carroll (1735-1815)
Prelate and Patriot

John Carroll led a religious minority group from the shadows of persecution into the bright light of American freedom.

Born into a distinguished family, he attended Jesuit schools in Maryland and in Flanders. There he entered the Society of Jesuit (1753). Carroll was ordained shortly before the Pope suppressed the Society of Jesus (1773). He returned home and ministered in Maryland. A diplomatic effort in Canada, on behalf of the revolutionary Continental Congress, brought him the regard of Benjamin Franklin. The elder statesman endorsed Carroll, who was chosen in 1784 as "Superior" of the missionary Church in America.

Carroll embarked on unifying the scattered Catholic communities. For the new nation, there must be a new diocese. Carroll was the natural choice to lead it, and he was consecrated a bishop on August 15, 1790, in England. His diocese included all states and territories until 1808, when four new dioceses were established; he then became an archbishop.

Portrait by Rembrandt Peale
(Courtesy Architect of the Capitol)

Besides dealing with pastoral and organizational challenges, he fostered a native clergy and education at all levels, including founding Georgetown Academy (later University) and welcoming Sulpicians to establish St. Mary's Seminary.

Respect for Carroll's wisdom and leadership crossed religious and geographic boundaries. He combined firmness with respect for liberty and shrewdness with kindness. He has justly been called the "father" of Catholicism in America.

So thought the priests, who petitioned Rome in 1788 for their own diocese, with their own bishop. Pope Pius VI consulted the cardinals responsible for mission territories, who agreed.

A papal decree established the Diocese of Baltimore in 1789, including all the United States of America and their territories. The Pope allowed a one-time-only privilege—the priests would elect their bishop. Their decision was clear: John Carroll, by a vote of 24 to 2. Carroll sailed to England in 1790, where he was ordained a bishop on August 15, the feast of the Assumption of the Blessed Virgin Mary.

Another provision in the Pope's decree had been "to erect...a Cathedral Church, inasmuch as the times and circumstances may allow." Catholic churches had been prohibited in colonial times. A Jesuit chapel in Newtown was built to look like a tobacco barn. Worshippers gathered in private homes or in simple "Mass houses." Baltimore's Mass house, called St. Peter's (begun in 1770) had been enlarged in 1784. It served as Carroll's "paltry" cathedral. When he had laid the foundations of the new diocese itself, Carroll began to plan a proper cathedral church. First and foremost a house of worship, it would also address the needs of the time.

• Catholicism was nearly invisible. The cathedral would stand upon the area's highest point.

• Catholics were marginalized. The cathedral would be their spiritual home.

• Catholics suffered from their fellow-citizens' suspicions that they were not truly American, that their total allegiance was to Rome. The cathedral would reflect an American spirit.

• Catholics had labored under restrictions, even oppression, as a religious minority. The cathedral would celebrate religious liberty.

By 1806 Bishop Carroll and the other trustees of the newly incorporated "Roman Catholic Congregation in Baltimore" had secured a site and were raising funds. It was time to lay the cornerstone for the nation's first Catholic cathedral.

St. Peter's Pro-cathedral (right) was depicted in 1801 by Thomas Ruckles.
Left of St. Peter is the rectory of St. Paul Episcopal Church.
(Photo courtesy of Associated Archives at St. Mary's Seminary and University)

AN ARCHITECTURAL MASTERPIECE

The "Father of American Architecture," B. Henry Latrobe (1764-1820), offered Bishop Carroll his services *pro bono*. The first truly professional architect in the new nation, Latrobe did much of the design work on the United States Capitol building, working with President Thomas Jefferson. Yet Baltimore's cathedral is considered his masterpiece.

Both Jefferson the gifted amateur and Latrobe the trained professional drew inspiration from the classic forms of ancient Greece and Rome.

(Photos by John Glover)

"I am a...Greek," Latrobe wrote to Jefferson. The neo-classical impulse did not duplicate the past but used it to create a new architectural style. The Capitol was unique at the time but evoked memories of Greco-Roman temples and law courts.

Light flows through the skylights and down into the rotunda. The ledge is the walkway around the oculus. A sculpted dove is now suspended from the dome's summit. (Photo by John Glover)

Neo-classical architecture honored the noble ideals inherited from the ancients. Democracy, born in Athens, was among the greatest of these ideals. The new American republic was launching a democratic experiment. The Baltimore cathedral makes a statement in the visual language of architecture; it affirms democracy and religious liberty.

It shares the style of the nation's Capitol; it is consciously American.

Using familiar Greek components, Latrobe designed a portico of fluted Ionic columns. They support a triangular pediment above the entrance, harking back to the façades of ancient temples.

Neo-classical principles govern the cathedral's interior, too. Symmetry, order and simple geometric forms shape the space: circles, triangles, right angles.

Space and light, rather than ornament, create a sense of grandeur. Barrel vaulting enhances the impression of height and solid regularity. Clear windows line the north and south walls, flooding the nave with light. For the neo-classicist, light represents human reason. While reason and order were basic principles among the new nation's founders, a long Christian tradition also associates light with faith and grace. The cathedral's use of light represents a very Catholic affirmation that reason and faith complement each other. They do not conflict.

Latrobe incorporated ancient Rome's distinctive architectural

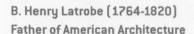

**B. Henry Latrobe (1764-1820)
Father of American Architecture**

The architect whose cathedral crowns Baltimore brought professional architecture and engineering to a new nation.

Born in England, B. Henry Latrobe studied in Germany and traveled through Europe, where he contemplated Gothic buildings and the emerging neo-classical style. Apprenticeships to an engineer and to an architect prepared him for professional service in London.

As a young widower, he began anew in America in 1796. Mary Elizabeth Hazlehurst, his second wife, balanced Latrobe's artistic temperament. Besides Lydia and Henry, from his first marriage, they had John H.B., Julia and Benjamin Henry.

The Bank of Philadelphia, Philadelphia's waterworks and other projects demonstrated Latrobe's skills, and President Thomas Jefferson appointed him Surveyor of the Public Buildings of the United States in 1803. His job included completing the nation's Capitol building, in trouble from faulty designs. Political pressures complicated enormous construction problems, but Latrobe's results were brilliant.

When Bishop John Carroll asked him to review a proposal for Baltimore's cathedral, Latrobe pointed out its flaws and volunteered his own services *pro bono*. He produced his masterpiece.

Construction stood still during the War of 1812, and Latrobe built steamboats in Pittsburgh. Trusting and optimistic, he was tricked and plunged into debt and depression. His energy returned with a commission to rebuild the Capitol, burned by the British. But his son Henry's death from yellow fever in New Orleans overwhelmed him. Latrobe resigned.

Baltimore welcomed the Latrobes in 1818. Archbishop Ambrose Marechal was bringing the cathedral to completion, and the architect was also involved in the Baltimore Exchange building.

Soon the family moved to New Orleans, to the waterworks project that Latrobe had initiated and Henry had directed. Father followed son, falling victim to yellow fever. B. Henry Latrobe died on September 3, 1820.

His legacy to the nation endures.

B. Henry Latrobe by Rembrandt Peale. (Courtesy of the Basilica of the Assumption Historic Trust, Inc.)

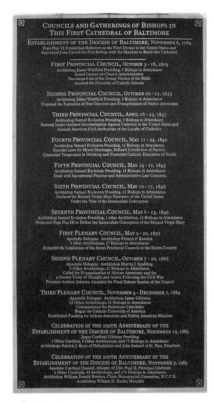

COUNCILS AND GATHERINGS OF BISHOPS IN
THIS FIRST CATHEDRAL OF BALTIMORE

ESTABLISHMENT OF THE DIOCESE OF BALTIMORE, NOVEMBER 6, 1789
Pope Pius VI Established Baltimore as the First Diocese in the United States and
Appointed John Carroll the First Bishop with the Mandate to Build this Cathedral

FIRST PROVINCIAL COUNCIL, OCTOBER 3 - 18, 1829
Archbishop James Whitfield Presiding, 5 Bishops in Attendance
Issued Decrees on Church Administration
Encouraged use of the Douay Version of the Bible
Asserted the Necessity of Catholic Schools

SECOND PROVINCIAL COUNCIL, OCTOBER 20 - 27, 1833
Archbishop James Whitfield Presiding, 9 Bishops in Attendance
Proposed the Formation of New Dioceses and Evangelization of Native Americans

THIRD PROVINCIAL COUNCIL, APRIL 16 - 23, 1837
Archbishop Samuel Eccleston Presiding, 9 Bishops in Attendance
Pastoral Letter Outlined Discrimination Against Catholics in the United States and
Assured American Civil Authorities of the Loyalty of Catholics

FOURTH PROVINCIAL COUNCIL, MAY 17 - 24, 1840
Archbishop Samuel Eccleston Presiding, 12 Bishops in Attendance
Enacted Laws for Mixed Marriages, Defined Jurisdiction of Pastors,
Counseled Temperance in Drinking and Promoted Catholic Education of Youth

FIFTH PROVINCIAL COUNCIL, MAY 14 - 21, 1843
Archbishop Samuel Eccleston Presiding, 15 Bishops in Attendance
Dealt with Sacramental Practice and Administrative Law Concerns

SIXTH PROVINCIAL COUNCIL, MAY 10 - 17, 1846
Archbishop Samuel Eccleston Presiding, 23 Bishops in Attendance
Declared the Blessed Virgin Mary Patroness of the United States
Under the Title of the Immaculate Conception

SEVENTH PROVINCIAL COUNCIL, MAY 6 - 13, 1849
Archbishop Samuel Eccleston Presiding, 1 other Archbishop, 23 Bishops in Attendance
Petitioned Pope Pius IX to Define the Immaculate Conception of the Blessed Virgin Mary

FIRST PLENARY COUNCIL, MAY 9 - 20, 1852
Apostolic Delegate: Archbishop Francis P. Kenrick
5 other Archbishops, 27 Bishops in Attendance
Extended the Legislation of the Seven Provincial Councils to the Entire Country

SECOND PLENARY COUNCIL, OCTOBER 7 - 20, 1866
Apostolic Delegate: Archbishop Martin J. Spalding
6 Other Archbishops, 37 Bishops in Attendance
Called for Evangelization of African Americans and for
a Greater Unity of Thought and Action Following the Civil War
President Andrew Johnson Attended the Final Solemn Session of the Council

THIRD PLENARY COUNCIL, NOVEMBER 9 - DECEMBER 7, 1884
Apostolic Delegate: Archbishop James Gibbons
13 Other Archbishops, 55 Bishops in Attendance
Commissioned the Baltimore Catechism
Began the Catholic University of America
Established Funding for African American and Native American Missions

CELEBRATION OF THE 100TH ANNIVERSARY OF THE
ESTABLISHMENT OF THE DIOCESE OF BALTIMORE, NOVEMBER 10, 1889
James Cardinal Gibbons Presiding
1 Other Cardinal, 8 Other Archbishops, and 75 Bishops in Attendance
Archbishops Patrick J. Ryan of Philadelphia and John Ireland of St. Paul, Preachers

CELEBRATION OF THE 200TH ANNIVERSARY OF THE
ESTABLISHMENT OF THE DIOCESE OF BALTIMORE, NOVEMBER 5, 1989
Agostino Cardinal Casaroli, delegate of John Paul II, Principal Celebrant
6 Other Cardinals, 33 Archbishops, and 270 Bishops in Attendance
Archbishop William Donald Borders, Chair, Bicentennial Committee, N.C.C.B.
Archbishop William H. Keeler, Homilist

*This plaque on the
northwest column of the
rotunda commemorates
historic gatherings
which took place in
the cathedral.
(Photo by John Glover).*

contribution, the dome. By this time, Renaissance and Baroque architects had raised the dome to the heights seen in St. Peter's Basilica in Rome and in St. Paul's Cathedral in London. Like them, the Capitol dome is elevated by high, colonnaded drums. The effect is to dominate the view of those who approach the building, to convey a sense of power.

Rome's Pantheon best exemplifies the ancient Roman dome. It rises gently, hardly visible to those approaching at close range. Such a dome has two functions. First, it surprises those who enter; they find the interior ascending to an unexpected height. Second, it brings in light from far above. Within the building, this dome creates an experience of awe. This is the type of dome that Latrobe chose to crown the cathedral, cross-tipped to denote its sacred space.

His conversations with President Thomas Jefferson had convinced Latrobe that skylights could work. They would be set into a wood-ribbed outer dome built above an inner brick-and-masonry dome. He learned from the technique of Philibert Delorme (1500/15-1570), who had used bolted pieces of laminated wood to span large spaces in the Halle au Blé, Paris. Latrobe's twenty-four skylights, each ten feet long, pierced the wooden outer dome. They cast light indirectly through an opening (*oculus*, Latin for eye) in the inner dome and down into the rotunda. The result was a soft light from far above, suggesting an unseen, heavenly source. To the brilliance of reason and faith, Latrobe had added a third, more mysterious effect of light: the sublime.

When completed, this American church would serve an American Catholic community. The cathedral would host the most significant

Bishops participating in the Second Plenary Council of Baltimore (1866) were photographed on the cathedral portico steps. (Photo courtesy of Associated Archives at St. Mary's Seminary and University)

events in the early development of the Church in the United States. For decades, almost all the bishops for the country's multiplying dioceses were ordained to the episcopate here.

Carroll had convened his first diocesan synod in St. Peter's Pro-cathedral in 1791. After 1821, such councils took place in the new cathedral. By then the country had other dioceses, whose bishops came to provincial councils convened by the Archbishop of Baltimore. After 1850, with several archdioceses established, the councils of the nation's bishops were "plenary." These early councils set directions that would affect the lives of American Catholics down to the present, a few of which follow.

• Seven Provincial Councils laid the foundations for unity in faith and uniformity in practice across the country. They established diocesan boundaries, promoted seminaries and dealt with issues of mixed marriage and the challenges to the Faith in the often anti-Catholic public schools. The Sixth (1846) named Mary, under the title of the Immaculate Conception, as patron of the USA. The Seventh (1849) petitioned the Pope to define Mary's Immaculate Conception as a teaching of the Church.

• First Plenary Council (1852) – called for a school in each parish and a seminary in each diocese; extended previous decrees of the Province of Baltimore to the nation; encouraged practices to reflect those of the universal Church; regulated Church administration.

• Second Plenary Council (1866) – put limitations on lay trustees of parishes; set standards for clergy behavior; encouraged religion classes for Catholic children attending public schools, high school seminaries and an explanatory, non-controversial style in addressing religious issues; discouraged long sermons and religiously mixed marriages. (President Andrew Johnson attended the closing.)

• Third Plenary Council (1884) – decided to establish a Catholic university; required attendance at Catholic schools; commissioned a catechism (Baltimore Catechism) and aid to "the missions among Indians and Negroes"; established holy days of obligation; initiated the causes of canonization for Kateri Tekakwitha, Isaac Jogues and René Goupil.

The seventh version of Latrobe's "Roman" design was the basis for the cathedral. (Courtesy of the Basilica of the Assumption Historic Trust, Inc.)

AN AMERICAN STORY: THE FIRST CENTURY

B Before ground was broken for Baltimore's cathedral, two serious issues had been addressed: location and financing. By 1796 the local church held title to six lots on "Philpot's Hill," in the fashionable southeast section of (as-yet-unincorporated) Baltimore town. A population shift led the congregation's trustees to consider building on St. Peter's hillside cemetery—after respectfully moving the deceased, of course.

Promises of respect for their beloved dead did not placate the living parishioners, however. Furthermore, they preferred a hilltop to a slope. Carroll's concern about financing the purchase of more land was met by pledges from other trustees and

B. Henry Latrobe presented the trustees with two cathedral designs, one described as "Gothic," one as "Roman." The trustees chose the "Roman" style. The cruciform floorplan called for a dome over the intersection of the nave and the transepts, which formed the "crossbar." Columns supporting a triangular pediment formed the west portico. The plan may have been influenced by memories of the Parisian "Pantheon" and of Lulworth Castle Chapel in England, where Carroll had been ordained a bishop.

John Carroll blessed the cornerstone on July 7, 1806. (Drawing by Fornerette, courtesy of Associated Archives at St. Mary's Seminary and University)

John Carroll blessed "the first stone of the Cathedral church, to be erected for the honor of Almighty God, under the title of Jesus and Mary," on July 7, 1806. In centuries-old tradition, the church would face east. The congregation at prayer, gazing upon the altar and apse, would also be looking toward the rising sun, toward Christ, the Light of the World.

by the leadership commitment of Sulpician Father William Dubourg, then president of St. Mary's College.

In March 1806, the trustees purchased the desired site from Colonel John Eager Howard for $20,571, payable in five installments.

The architect congratulated the trustees "on the superior locality of your building." Its prominence would place the cathedral at the pinnacle of Baltimore's skyline, visible from the bay.

Progress on the foundations went slowly, stone upon stone from the Acquia Island (Virginia) sandstone quarries. Brick walls with hammered granite panels and trim from Ellicott City quarries rose in 1809 and 1810. Rhythmic barrel vaulting lifted the side aisles with a feeling of light and space.

The winning lottery ticket resulted in a major increase in the building fund. (Courtesy of the Basilica of the Assumption Historic Trust, Inc.)

A series of seven plans grew out of Latrobe's proposal, which was continually being modified. Latrobe and Carroll, both well-traveled in Europe, may have been the only people involved who could even imagine a building of the scale and majesty envisioned here. None of the trustees had their experience, nor did the members of the committee overseeing the construction. George Rohrbach, the builder, could not even read the plans correctly. He held them upside down, confusing the vaulting with the foundation.

Trustee John Hillen III, committee chairman, directed Rohrbach to make unauthorized changes. The Hillen-Rohrbach changes drove Latrobe to resign three times. Only Carroll's tact soothed the architect's anger. Nonetheless, Latrobe had to keep adjusting to compensate for the committee's demands and Rohrbach's errors. He must have sighed as he wrote, "Let the alteration be made. I will devote the necessary time to a new design, and hope it shall succeed. I do not see how at present, but the resources of art are infinite."

After Hillen resigned, St. Peter's rector Father Francis Beeston was Latrobe's liaison. From then on Rohrbach followed the architect's plans. Even so, there were further

Leonard Neale was the second archbishop of Baltimore. St. Peter's Pro-cathedral is seen through the window. (By permission of the Georgetown University Archives)

The Assumption

From very early times, Christians have believed that Jesus' mother Mary was "assumed" into heaven after her death. Art as well as theology paints the picture: Mary's body taken by God into eternal life. The Creed professes, "I believe in...the resurrection of the body." Belief in the Assumption asserts that Mary is the first to receive this grace, which is the destiny of all human beings. Pope Pius XII formally declared this teaching in 1950.

revisions. For example, the trustees wanted wider aisles, and Carroll wanted better visibility from aisles to altar. The rotunda was widened, with its supportive piers on a diagonal.

Toward the end of the project, the trustees would write to their departing architect, "Objections were sometimes made to parts of your plans, the propriety and connection of which [the trustees'] inexperience did not permit them at the time to discern clearly; but now that the various details of the building form one grand and beautiful whole, they are fully convinced of the propriety of having...given way to your greater experience and better judgment.... [Y]ou have erected the most splendid temple on this side of the Atlantic...."

Fund-raising was an on-going responsibility for Bishop Carroll. At their very first meeting (December 29, 1795), the trustees authorized "subscriptions," or financial pledges, to purchase property. Carroll appealed to every Catholic family in the country to contribute one dollar a year for four years. In 1803 a public lottery raised $30,000. And the winner was...Bishop Carroll! He turned over the $20,000 prize directly to the building fund.

By 1810 the trustees were raising funds by the advance "sale" of pews, a common practice at the time, allowing families exclusive use of "their" pews. Lack of funds interrupted the building process at the end of 1810. The War of 1812 extended the delay. No more work was done during Carroll's lifetime. At his death in 1815, his cathedral dream was unrealized: a shell boarded up for the winter.

The trustees resumed work in early 1817, despite the absence of the sickly Archbishop Leonard Neale, Carroll's successor. They hired James Hayden to supervise construction. In October 1818 Latrobe was present for the ceremonial driving of the four last bricks into the curbing around the oculus, the central opening of the inner dome.

Step by step, roofing covered the nave and sanctuary, forming shallow "saucer domes." Galleries went up in the two transepts. The choir and organ would occupy the north gallery. The upper south gallery came to be called "the Sisters' gallery." Devotional altars honored Jesus as the Good Shepherd and Mary, his mother, one at the head of each aisle in the triangular space facing into the rotunda.

The third Archbishop of Baltimore, the Sulpician Ambrose Maréchal, S.S., was a vigorous leader of the cathedral project. A native of France, Maréchal made the most of his European contacts. He appealed to the French Cardinal Joseph Fesch for religious art and to Charles Nerinckx, from Belgium, for church goods. His former seminary students from Marseilles contributed the altar and other furnishings.

Maréchal dedicated the Cathedral of the Assumption of the Blessed Virgin Mary on May 31, 1821, assisted by Bishops John Lefevre de Cheverus of Boston and Henry Conwell of Philadelphia. The cathedral was jammed with people; thousands more came but could not be admitted. This was the grandest event that Baltimore had ever witnessed. Although the towers were unfinished, no portico covered the west door, and several interior features remained incomplete, the new cathedral evoked awe.

Despite the naming of "Jesus and Mary" at the cornerstone-laying in 1806, at some point the Assumption had emerged as the cathedral's title. The reason may lie in the date of Carroll's ordination as Baltimore's bishop: August 15, the feast of the Assumption. Mary appears on his

Archbishop Ambrose Maréchal, S.S., brought the cathedral to completion in 1821. (Courtesy of the Basilica of the Assumption Historic Trust, Inc.)

Archbishop James Whitfield had the south tower built. (Courtesy of the Basilica of the Assumption Historic Trust, Inc.)

Archbishop Samuel Eccleston led the construction of the cathedral's second tower, completed furnishings, and extended the west gallery. (Courtesy of the Basilica of the Assumption Historic Trust, Inc.)

coat of arms, surrounded by stars. The work continued, as funds became available and leaders moved the process forward. Archbishop James Whitfield, who succeeded Maréchal, called upon the clergy to complete the towers. Under the direction of John H. B. Latrobe, the architect's son, the south tower was finished in 1831. A 3500-pound bell, cast in France, was installed in it in honor of Maréchal, donated by one of his former pupils. A smaller bell was mounted at the same time. The clock, from Paris, was installed in the south tower in 1866.

The sexton (caretaker) lived in a brick house just north of the cathedral, built in 1840/41.

The north tower went up in 1837, during the episcopacy of Archbishop Samuel Eccleston. The younger Latrobe remarked on the effect of the two slender towers "to lighten by contrast" the dome's massiveness. Latrobe senior had designed their onion-shaped domes, tipped with slender crosses. Moscow's Church of the Assumption may have inspired this unusual shape.

Eccleston also raised the sanctuary's floor-level and enlarged the west gallery, to which Black worshippers were relegated, in the lower tier. Confessionals and stoves were installed in 1834 and 1838, respectively. In 1841 iron fencing designed by Robert C. Long, Jr., surrounded the grounds.

Leakage problems were becoming apparent in the 1840s. To remedy the situation, a shed-style layer was added on top of the roof in 1858. This addition reduced the dome's prominence above the roof.

The cathedral interior is seen from the perspective of the west gallery toward the east apse, in this early engraving. (Engraving courtesy of Associated Archives at St. Mary's Seminary and University)

One major feature was still lacking: the west portico. John H. B. Latrobe submitted plans for its foundation, which was laid in 1841. Almost two more decades passed until Archbishop Francis P. Kenrick undertook the portico itself. The Civil War delayed fund-raising and delivery of materials. Tan New Brunswick freestone for the columns was coming from Nova Scotia. By 1863, ten fluted columns with Ionic capitals were standing, topped by an iron ceiling under the Greek pediment. The portico brought the cathedral to completion, more than half a century after the cornerstone had been laid.

Not till 1876 was the debt retired. Now the cathedral's solemn consecration could take place. On May 25, the feast of the Ascension, Archbishop James Roosevelt Bayley presided at the six-and-a-half-hour ceremony attended by thousands, including spectators lining Cathedral and Mulberry Streets.

The cathedral's major bell was donated by a former pupil of Archbishop Maréchal. (Photo by John Glover)

The cathedral lacked its intended portico until the 1860s. (Engraving courtesy of Associated Archives at St. Mary's Seminary and University)

Over time, the purity of Latrobe's and Carroll's concepts was lost, at least inside the building. With influences from European churches, intensity replaced the restrained, almost austere original style. In 1865, before the Second Plenary Council, Archbishop Martin J. Spalding wanted the cathedral "handsomely fitted up and adorned." He had the sanctuary columns painted in imitation of red Sienna marble. Colorful paintings substituted imagery for the effects of light. An inscription in the frieze imitated that of St. Peter's Basilica in Rome, though its English spoke to an American congregation: THE HOUSE OF GOD, WHICH IS THE CHURCH OF GOD, THE PILLAR AND GROUND OF TRUTH. ONE LORD, ONE FAITH, ONE BAPTISM. (It was replaced in 1961 by a Latin verse from the Magnificat, Mary's hymn in Luke 1.)

In the 1860s geometric tiles were laid over the herringbone brickwork floor, which had been a temporary concession to finances during the cathedral's construction.

The changes were structural, too. Stained glass was inserted into a half-circle window opened above

26

the altar. A tripartite window cut above the west door, probably in 1867, marred the exterior. Four Ionic columns were removed from between the narthex (vestibule) and the nave. The west gallery was enlarged for pews.

Embellishment continued. Painted Stations of the Cross, donated by Captain William Marshall Boone, lined the walls in 1878. Large canvases given to Maréchal by French kings were mounted in the nave rear. Archbishop (later Cardinal) James Gibbons repainted and laid marble in the sanctuary in 1879. The city's great fire of 1873 had threatened the cathedral; marble was part of an effort at fireproofing. The side altars were repositioned in the transepts. A sacristy was added on the north side of the sanctuary. The younger Latrobe protested inconsistencies that would spoil his father's building, and Gibbons tried to harmonize the new with the old.

As the Catholic population in America mushroomed, so did new dioceses. Church councils and even the local clergy outgrew the cathedral's sanctuary. Ninety-six prelates attended the 1889 centennial of the United States hierarchy. Cardinal Gibbons met this need by enlarging the sanctuary, extending it eastward by about thirty-four feet in 1890. Architect Frank J. Baldwin preserved elements of Latrobe's design in the curved apse wall marked by six Ionic columns. The altar was moved to the point of the original east wall, and the half-circle saucer dome above it was expanded

into a full circle. Two side altars were added in the extended apse, one dedicated to St. Michael and one to St. James the Less.

By January 1899 electricity was lighting the interior.

Archbishop Martin J. Spalding had the cathedral redecorated for the Second Plenary Council (1865). (Courtesy of the Basilica of the Assumption Historic Trust, Inc.)

Archbishop James Roosevelt Bayley solemnly consecrated the cathedral on May 25, 1876. (Courtesy of the Basilica of the Assumption Historic Trust, Inc.)

Saint James the less holds a book representing the New Testament and a club representing his martyrdom. (Photo by John Glover)

ENDURANCE, EMBELLISHMENT, EMINENCE: THE SECOND CENTURY

A A building that survives two centuries of shifting taste and styles might be utterly transformed. Not so with this cathedral! Its monumental quality, its architectural distinction, its beauty have endured a saga of alterations.

In preparation for the cathedral's 1906 centennial, the dome's exterior gleamed with the addition of gold leaf. Another interior redecoration continued the Italian Renaissance style begun in 1865. Gold rosettes on a field of blue adorned the vaults and domes. Symbolizing the Holy Spirit, a dove sculpted within a gilded wooden sunburst was suspended under the great dome. Murals with Marian themes were painted in the two saucer domes—the Annunciation over the altar and the Assumption over the nave. Behind the main altar, the Transfiguration of Jesus was painted in a half-dome supported by the six Ionic, imitation-marble columns set against the east wall. Grecian marble replaced mahogany for a new altar railing.

At the cathedral in 1932, the Oblate Sisters of Providence celebrated the centennial of their foundation in Baltimore by Mother Mary Lange. Archbishop Michael J. Curley stands among the Sisters. (Photo courtesy of the Basilica of the Assumption Historic Trust, Inc.)

The 1940s saw major changes to structure and decor which took the cathedral further from its historic integrity. The deteriorating skylights were removed, their openings boarded up. With the closure of the skylights, the interior grew darker. Gray paint on the walls and green Cardiff marble on the floor contributed to the effect. Archbishop Michael Curley led these changes, carried out by Rambusch Decorating Company of New York, church specialists. Two doors were added, flanking the main entrance.

🔹 *Archbishop Francis P. Keough laid the cornerstone of the new Cathedral of Mary Our Queen in 1954. (Photos courtesy of Associated Archives at St. Mary's Seminary and Historic Trust, Inc. and Associated Archives at St. Mary's Seminary and University)*

🔹 *Cardinal Lawrence Sheehan participated in the Second Vatican Council and adjusted the basilica to its liturgical directives. (Photos courtesy of Associated Archives at St. Mary's Seminary and Historic Trust, Inc. and Associated Archives at St. Mary's Seminary and University)*

🔹 *Archbishop Williams D. Borders led the formation of the Basilica of the Assumption Historic Trust, Inc., in 1976. (Photos courtesy of Associated Archives at St. Mary's Seminary and Historic Trust, Inc. and Associated Archives at St. Mary's Seminary and University)*

Most dramatic was the introduction of stained glass into the windows, in imitation of European churches. Each nave window combined a prototype from the Hebrew Scriptures with the lives of Jesus and Mary and, at the bottom, an aspect of the Church in America. Though inspiring, the windows were inconsistent with the architecture.

By mid-century the Basilica could no longer serve the needs of the diocese, because of both growth and demographic shifts. In 1954, Archbishop Francis P. Keough laid the cornerstone of the Cathedral of Mary Our Queen, which was consecrated in 1959. The two then became co-cathedrals.

The early 1960s saw an exterior cleaning and another redecoration. When the Second Vatican Council called for liturgical renewal, church buildings underwent adjustments to foster full, conscious and active participation in the Mass. Cardinal Lawrence Sheehan implemented this teaching. The altar of sacrifice was moved closer to the people.

The cathedral's historic role has merited special recognition at every level. Pope Pius XI declared it a minor basilica in 1937. This designation creates a special relationship between an eminent church and the Pope. Two ceremonial items mark a basilica's rank: a red-and-gold-striped caponium (umbrella, or ombrellino) and a tintinabulum (bell on a pole), both used in papal processions. The United States Department of the Interior named the Basilica a National Historic Landmark in 1972. The National Conference of Catholic Bishops designated it a National Shrine in 1993.

Recognizing the particular needs of an architectural treasure, Archbishop William D. Borders led the formation of the Basilica of the Assumption Historic Trust, Inc., in 1976. This non-profit corporation undertook to ensure the preservation of the Basilica for future generations, a testimony in stone to the ideals of its builders and of two centuries of Catholics.

Momentous events continue to unfold. The bicentennial of the American hierarchy was observed within these hallowed walls in 1989, with Archbishop (later Cardinal) William Keeler presiding. The Basilica welcomed Pope John Paul II in 1995 and Mother Teresa of Calcutta in 1996.

Cardinal Keeler's ecumenical leadership led to other historic moments. For the first time in the United States, in 1997 an Orthodox Patriarch—Ecumenical Patriarch Bartholomew of Constantinople—presided and preached in a Roman Catholic cathedral. Marking the Great Jubilee of 2000, the Basilica hosted Jewish, Christian, Muslim and other religious leaders for The Creation Concert, conducted by Maestro Gilbert Levine with

The bishops of the United States celebrated the Eucharist in the Basilica for the bicentennial of the nation's episcopate in 1989. Cardinal Keeler is at the center. (Photo courtesy of Associated Archives at St. Mary's Seminary and University)

the Philharmonia Orchestra and Chorus of London. This was the first of an international Jubilee series. Also in 2000, members of the International Commission for Theological Dialogue between the Catholic and Orthodox Churches gathered here for the Eucharist.

Pope John Paul II visits the Basilica on October 8, 1995. (Photo courtesy of the Basilica of the Assumption Historic Trust, Inc.)

Mother (now Blessed) Teresa of Calcutta addresses a congregation including Missionaries of Charity on her visit to the Basilica on May 29, 1996. (Photo courtesy of the Basilica of the Assumption Historic Trust, Inc.)

The Creation Concert in the Basilica introduced the new millennium with an international, ecumenical musical event. (Photo courtesy of the Basilica of the Assumption Historic Trust, Inc.)

RESTORING THE LIGHT: THE THIRD CENTURY

Pope John Paul II welcomes Cardinal William Keeler in Vatican City on October 18, 2001. The Cardinal and a delegation from the Basilica of the Assumption Historic Trust presented the restoration plans to the Pope. (Photo by permission of L'Osservatore Romano)

B Beautiful. Impressive. Historic. Old. Two hundred years old.

The centuries had taken a toll on the Basilica's structure and on its infrastructure. Cardinal Keeler saw the need to address the problems. To neglect them would have spelled death for the venerable building. This symbol of faith and of religious freedom could not be allowed to disintegrate. The Basilica's mission had to continue. Because its original concept spoke so authentically of religious freedom in America, its architectural integrity would be restored. Adjustments would make it more welcoming to visitors, allowing

better circulation through the church and access to the undercroft.

Once again, a prelate of Baltimore called upon the generosity of those who appreciate the importance of this great building. The Historic Trust led the way, engaging top architectural advice. From a comprehensive professional assessment conducted by John G. Waite Associates, plans emerged, and from plans, action. A delegation of Trustees presented the results of the study to Pope John Paul II in Rome on October 18, 2001, and received his blessing. Work on the $32,000,000 restoration began in April 2004, under the

comprehensive direction of Henry H. Lewis, Contractors. The Basilica closed on November 21, 2004, not to reopen until November 4, 2006. Maryland's Governor Robert L. Ehrlich, Jr., declared 2006 "The Year of the Baltimore Basilica," and both houses of the General Assembly passed resolutions of congratulations. Accepting these proclamations on March 31, Cardinal Keeler recalled that the State had in 1795 approved "the fundraising and construction for the first great metropolitan cathedral in the newly formed United States. In the two centuries since, the Basilica has been a place of worship for a pope and saints, but just as important, it's been the spiritual home for generations of Maryland Catholics, who have faithfully come through the Basilica doors seeking comfort, inspiration, and celebration."

STRUCTURAL INTEGRITY
THE EXTERIOR

For two years, scaffolding was a familiar sight along Cathedral and Mulberry Streets. Specialists were hard at work blending preservation with historic restoration. Cleaning, painting and tuck-pointing are standard upkeep on masonry. This work goes further. The contour of the new mortar has the additional advantage of matching the original. New and repaired stucco work protects and brightens the exterior. All damaged features and surfaces have been returned to their original forms. The crosses atop towers and dome shine with new gold paint.

The finely crafted iron railing around the building went to Alabama. There the Robert C. Long, Jr., fence was cleaned and rebuilt, with replacement pieces cast as necessary.

In the portico, a black-and-white checkerboard pattern restores the 1840s look of the floor. Slate and white marble paving stones replace the

(Photo by William Bernard)

surface laid in the 1940s. The columns had to be cleaned and re-stained to match the Acquia stone of the walls. The portico's cast-iron ceiling panels needed restoration too. Under the roof, the window added in the 1860s has been closed, restoring Latrobe's intended façade. The original main door remains in place.

Latrobe's intended parapet between the two towers has at last been built. This finishing touch to the architect's plan unites the towers with the portico roof. The parapet was not constructed with the towers in the 1830s.

Ethlyn Fitzpatrick does repointing in the portico area. (Photo by William Bernard)

On the roof some of the most significant restoration has returned the Basilica's original contours. A raised shed roof had been installed over the original roof. With the covering now stripped away, the dome once more has its intended profile above the roof.

Remnants of the earliest wood shingles were discovered over the transepts, hidden by the later covering. New cedar shingles now assure that the roof looks much as it did in the nineteenth century. Lower parapets and historically

(Photo by John Glover)

accurate lead flashings also recreate the look of 1821.

Urgent repairs addressed severe problems of deterioration. Leakage and disintegrating materials threatened damage to paint and fixtures inside. Among the safety issues, brittle copper risked failure

in the lightning protection system, and corrosion in the snow-guards risked dumping heavy snow below. The dome's lead coating was heavily weathered and pitted, the copper surface unprotected. New cladding and replacement fixtures now protect the building's integrity.

MYSTERIOUS LIGHT
OPENING THE GREAT DOME

Opening the view through the dome into the rotunda meant opening a pathway for light. (Photo by William Bernard)

N No part of the Basilica is more powerful than its great double-shell dome. No aspect of the restoration was more important than reopening this magnificent source of light. It was the crowning feature of Latrobe's genius. Recrafted with wood lathe and lime plaster, twenty-four skylights in the

Perched on the dome, Phil Davis works on one of the newly opened skylights. (Photo by William Bernard)

Light from the skylights enters by the oculus and illuminates the dome interior. (Photo by John Glover)

dome's outer shell once again illuminate the rotunda.

Through the skylights daylight passes onto the inner dome, is reflected back to the curvature of the shell, is reflected again and enters the rotunda through the oculus. Latrobe designed the skylights so that only glimpses of them are visible from below. The source of the light thus remains mysterious (*lumière mystéricuse*), a sublime effect. The restored dome fills the rotunda with the architect's intended "mass of central light."

On the dome's interior, decorated coffers lighten the structure's actual weight and the impression it conveys to those below. A glance up through the oculus reveals a large rosette, like those in the coffers, suspended from the outer dome. Just above the oculus, under the rosette, hangs a dove carved in basswood, a newly commissioned work of art. It symbolizes the Holy Spirit, source of light and life for the Church. Sculptor Robert S. Thuman designed the figure as though the dove were gliding to a place of rest above God's people gathered here.

RECOVERING THE VISION
INSIDE THE BASILICA

Rhythmic geometric forms provide variety of line and space. The view here is from the west gallery into the rotunda (left) and the vaulting of the south ambulatory (right). (Photo by John Glover)

The rotunda is the powerful central force of the cathedral's interior. Supporting the dome, high arches spring from a strong cornice atop massive piers.

The arches pierce a tall drum that has gone through several artistic schemes, including a mural portraying the life of Mary. Inscriptions previously filled the frieze. In its simplicity, this area again functions as an architectural, not a decorative element, strong rather than ornamental.

An historic paintings on the rotunda surface is partially revealed, long hidden behind plaster and framework. This represents the evangelist Matthew. (Photo by William Bernard)

A surprising discovery during the restoration has given the rotunda a new—but old—look. As restoration architect Stephen F. Reilly of John G. Waite, Associates, tapped along the rotunda surface in 2005, he heard a hollow sound. Further exploration revealed a plaster and wooden encapsulation and, under that, rectangular paintings dating to 1865. The rediscovered images painted by Philip Nengel and Hubert Schmidt symbolize the evangelists with traditional figures suggested by the biblical book

This ionic-style capital is one of the four atop new columns marking the transition between narthex and nave. (Photo by John Glover)

of Ezekiel (1:10) and the Book of Revelation (4:7): an angel for Matthew, a lion for Mark, an ox for Luke and an eagle for John. Created with distempered water-based paint, each about 8'x11', the works were well preserved but required some restoration.

The nave is not a mere anteroom to the rotunda. It is the longest line of the architectural Roman

cross. From the outside, its doors open into a narthex under the west gallery. Passing through this vestibule, one enters the body of the church.

The west gallery has been returned to its earliest dimensions with the removal of the 1867 extension, a balcony. Several revelations occurred in the process, including two half-domes which had been covered in 1879. Another discovery is that original structural components—a forty-foot cast-iron composite support beam and oak timbers—not only survive but survive in good condition.

Since the balcony had blocked the view of the nave's western vaulting, the full spatial effect of the nave is once more visible. A rear ambulatory (walkway) crosses under the vaulting. Four ornamental Ionic columns and two pilasters placed here are replicas; the originals were removed in the 1860s. These accentuate Latrobe's transition between the narthex and the ambulatory.

A vivid freshness characterizes the symbol of the evangelist Mark after restoration. (Photo by John Glover)

The carved white marble baptismal font in the northwest ambulatory corner is one of the gifts made to Maréchal in 1820.

The center aisle leads forward to an open area. Here a saucer dome gives the nave its own sense of significant space. A new painting of the Assumption of Mary in its center introduces the Basilica's Marian theme in a style consistent with the nineteenth century.

The Basilica by the Numbers

Length (exterior*, including portico and steps) – 226′

Length from west door to exterior of east wall – 192′

Width in nave, west (interior,** under saucer dome) – 70′

Width at transepts (exterior, including vestibules) – 115′

Height from floor to top of outer dome – 87′

Diameter of base of dome steps – 75′

Diameter of oculus – 22′

Height of towers from brick paving to top of cross – c. 120′

* from outer surface to outer surface

** from inner surface to inner surface

Mary's Assumption crowns the saucer dome in the west end of the nave. (Photo by John Glover)

punctuated by smaller triangular recesses.

Tall windows, three in both the north and the south walls, introduce light. The windows face each other, seen between the arches that mark off the side aisles. Their fan-shaped top sections harmonize with the arches and vaulting. Their clear glass replaces stained glass from the 1940s and restores both light and simplicity. The repainted walls reflect the restored brightness in tones ranging from off-white to beige as sunlight shifts.

Column capitals, cornices, rosettes and moldings throughout the interior now look as they did when the Cathedral opened, thanks to repairs, replications and repainting. Repairing water damage and reconstructing design features involved over 10,000 square feet of three-coat plasterwork.

It draws upon artistic traditions, especially Tiepolo's Assumption. Mary's facial features exemplify a portrait-style realism. A clay-based adhesive fastens the canvas, which has a fifteen-foot diameter, to the dome surface. Twelve circular coffers with rosettes ring the shallow dome,

The windows are once again clear avenues of light. (Photo by John Glover)

Vaulting over the side aisles matches the vaulting at the nave's west end, just inside the entrance. Square coffers provide a decorative counterpoint to the building's many architectural curves. An Ionic entablature surrounds the nave. Its strong horizontal provides both balance and energy, as from it springs the vaulting. From a lower entablature spring the arches to the side aisles. This rhythm of curved and straight lines has defined the structure through all its decorative variations. The continuity of the

cornice all around the building has been restored across the west gallery.

Creamy white marble pavers, quarried in Colorado and shaped in Georgia, enhance the Basilica's brightness. The green marble laid in the 1940s had to be removed and replaced to accommodate ductwork for the new heating and air-conditioning systems, laid under the main floor.

New pews and confessionals are consistent with the earliest wood furnishings; parts are painted and parts treated with a mahogany stain.

Twelve new crosses and candle-sconces on the walls and pilasters denote that this is a solemnly consecrated church. They replace the crosses hung in 1876. Consecration candles are lighted each year on the anniversary of the Basilica's consecration (May 25) and for other solemn ceremonies.

Six new chandeliers and six new lanterns in bronze replicate early nineteenth-century fixtures. Custom-crafted, they replace the previous, worn-out equipment.

The crossbar of the architectural cross forms transepts, one on either side of the rotunda, marked off by Ionic columns. The transept galleries were extended in 1867, crowding into the rotunda. The recent restoration has drawn them back to their original dimensions, allowing the great rotunda its full circumference. The organ and seating for the choir occupy the gallery in the north transept. The south transept is an entrance, with a gallery and pews above. Spiral staircases lead to the galleries in both transepts.

The sanctuary has undergone more evolution than any other part of the church. It occupies the "head" of the architectural cross. That space was almost doubled by the extension of 1890. Six engaged Ionic columns

The west gallery has been returned to its original depth. It no longer obscures the view of the vaulting over the west ambulatory. (Photo by John Glover)

line the semicircular apse behind the sanctuary furnishings.

A painting of Christ's Ascension into heaven fills the saucer dome over the center of the sanctuary. This Christological theme is more appropriate above the altar than the previous Assumption painting of 1962. Christ's face blends features drawn from centuries of Western art. To harmonize with the architectural coffers, painted *trompe l'œil* replicas decorate the pendentives under this dome. The painting and other decorative work parallel the features of the nave dome.

From the nave entrance, a series of lighted spaces draws the eye forward to the altar. This photo shows the work in progress, during the restoration. (Photo by John Glover)

The full sanctuary includes vaulted areas on either side of the dome, originally enclosed as the vestry (south) and sacristy (north). These were opened in 1890. Windows added on the south side at that time match those of the nave. A plaque commemorating the Third Plenary Council (1884) hangs on the south wall. Nearby is the caponium, the umbrella that denotes a papal basilica.

On the north side hangs a portrait of Cardinal Gibbons, painted by Marie Keller and donated by the Shriver family. The tintinnabulum (bell used in a basilica's papal processions) stands here. A doorway leads to the sacristy, which was added in 1879. It houses the vestments, liturgical vessels and other items used in religious services.

Christ's Ascension into heaven is the subject of the mural in the saucer dome above the altar. (Photo by John Glover)

the prayer of all the people, the altar was adjusted so that the priest could face the congregation. The sanctuary has now been raised further to a level two feet above the main floor, to enhance visibility.

The new marble pulpit, with a new gilded baldachino (canopy-like structure), replicates the original pulpit. Here Scripture is proclaimed and sermons are preached. Today's acoustic technology overcomes the problems that merited for the 1821 pulpit the joking title of "the tomb of eloquence."

The cathedra (bishop's ceremonial chair) recalls the Basilica's original function. From this chair archbishops from Maréchal to Curley presided over the Archdiocese of Baltimore. A century ago a marble chair replaced it. Reconditioned and reupholstered, the first cathedra now faces the congregation under an ornate new baldachino. The word *cathedral* comes from the cathedra in the

A church's spiritual centerpoint is the altar. The Basilica's new white marble altar stands directly under the sanctuary dome. It replaces the temporary wooden altar installed after the Second Vatican Council (1962-1965). Then, with the understanding of the Eucharist as

bishop's church (here a co-cathedral). The red hat once worn by Cardinal Gibbons hangs near the cathedra. Traditional practice is for a cardinal's hat to hang in his cathedral until the hat crumbles to dust.

The marble high altar of 1821, removed in the 1940s, has been replicated from old photographs. This careful replication serves as the altar of reservation for the Blessed Sacrament. Here the Body of Christ, in the form of the bread consecrated during the Eucharist, is reserved to be taken to the sick and for private devotion between Eucharistic celebrations. Images of two cherubs adorn the new marble tabernacle, which is built into the altar. The rococo-style lamp hanging before the altar testifies to the presence of Christ, as it has since 1849. The lamp's elaborate gilded bronze shines with renewed brilliance.

Two wooden sculptures of kneeling angels flank the altar of reservation. These figures were relegated to the

crypt in the 1930s. Master woodworker James Adajian used ultraviolet technology to discover seventeen layers of white paint, which he removed to get to the base layer before applying an historically accurate finish. Ed Milburn, a gilder, finished the surfaces. For one angel, whose feet had been lost, Adajian carved replacements. Both artisans are Baltimoreans. The angels now resume the function they had at the cathedral's beginning: symbolizing adoration for Christ present in the Blessed Sacrament.

The altar of reservation stands at the point of the original east wall. Visitors can pass behind it on a devotional circuit of the cathedral.

A railing separates the sanctuary from the nave. Like the 1820s railing, it is wood painted white, with mahogany trim. It stands farther east than its predecessor, so as not to cut into the rotunda, and surrounds the raised sanctuary on three sides. The addition of side sections marks out

an ambulatory between the sanctuary and the devotional shrines along the walls.

The high altar provides the sacred space for reservation of the Blessed Sacrament. (Photo by John Glover)

DEVOTIONAL TREASURES

If the Basilica's liturgical life takes place on an axis from entrance to apse, its devotional life surrounds it, along the walls.

Historic French paintings have returned to the nave after decades in obscurity. Saint (King) Louis IX is the subject of one large canvas. With his chaplain, his armor-bearer and a soldier, he buries a plague-stricken soldier before the walls of Tunis. King Louis XVIII commissioned this painting by Baron Charles de

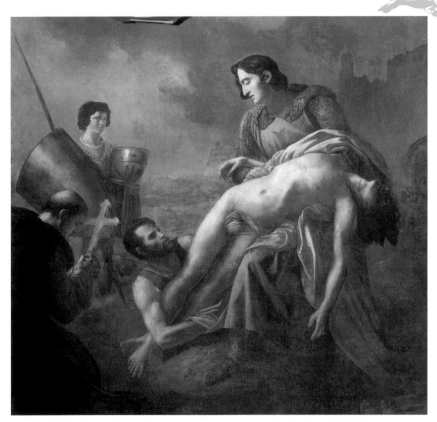

The painting of St. Louis burying a soldier is a study in compassion, painted by Baron Charles de Steuben. It hangs in the west ambulatory. (Photo by John Glover)

The Society of Jesus is recalled by its emblem, the Greek monogram for the name of Jesus. (Photo by John Glover)

Mary, titled "the Immaculate Conception," is represented by this marble statue. (Photo by John Glover)

Steuben as a gift to the cathedral. It portrays the monarch as a model of compassion, performing one of the corporal works of mercy. King Louis hangs on the west nave wall, at the end of the north aisle.

A moving *Pietà* painted by Baron Pierre Narcisse Guérin is on the south side. Mary of Magdala and John lament over the body of Jesus, which Joseph of Arimathea and Nicodemus have just removed from the cross. King Louis XVIII commissioned this painting for the cathedral; his successor King Charles X actually made the gift.

The seal of the Society of Jesus appears in the ambulatory's southwest corner. Its distinctive IHS is a monogram of the name Jesus in Greek, erected in honor of Baltimore's two first archbishops.

Both Carroll and Neale had been Jesuits before the Society was suppressed in 1773. Both fostered its partial restoration in the United States in 1805. (Universal restoration took place in 1814.)

Vivid Stations of the Cross circle the church, starting from the sacristy door. These paintings on wood by an unknown artist were a gift from Captain William Marshall Boone in 1878. They have spent more than a half-century in the basement. Carefully restored, they once more help Christians to accompany Jesus spiritually from his condemnation by Pilate to his crucifixion and burial.

Shrines to Mary and Joseph occupy triangular spaces on either side of the sanctuary, near the transepts. On the north side a white marble figure honors Mary under her title of the Immaculate Conception, patron saint of the United States. The Basilica has a unique connection with this Marian title. The Seventh

Provincial Council of Baltimore, meeting here in 1849, petitioned Pope Pius IX to declare this teaching, long held within the Church. In 1854 he did so, proclaiming the belief that God preserved Mary from sin (immaculate) from the first moment of her life (conception) to prepare her for her role in salvation history as Jesus' mother. In a corresponding space on the south side is a white marble statue of Saint Joseph holding the Child Jesus. Both statues were carved in Italy.

Memorial features recall historic figures and events in the Basilica's life. Archbishop John Carroll's memorial, a white marble bust, recalls the first great leader of the Church in America, the builder of this cathedral. It is in the south transept. The archbishops who have followed Carroll are named, with him, on a new commemorative panel near his memorial. Nearby a bronze plaque commemorates the 1936 visit of then-Cardinal Eugenio Pacelli, later Pope Pius XII.

Saint Joseph holds the Child Jesus as depicted in this marble statue. (Photo by John Glover)

In the north transept is a memorial to Cardinal James Gibbons, among the towering leaders of American Catholicism. Baptized in this cathedral, he returned to preach at its solemn consecration. His tenure as archbishop (1877-1921, cardinal in 1886) was the longest among Baltimore's prelates.

Historical markers mounted on two of the dome piers commemorate the bishops consecrated in this cathedral (SW pier) and all the Church councils held here (NW pier). Pope John Paul II blessed the latter when he visited the Basilica in 1995.

A statue of Pope John Paul II on the north wall, between the confessionals, recalls the papal visit. *The Blessing*, a bronze sculpture by Kris Parmele, portrays another visitor, Blessed Teresa of Calcutta, along the south wall. Cardinal

Lawrence Sheehan (1961–1974) is honored in the west ambulatory (north side), with a white Vermont marble bust sculpted by Nate Risteen.

A white marble statue of Saint Michael the Archangel stands in a niche in the east wall, on the south side. His drawn sword shows him as God's agent in a cosmic battle against evil. Saint James the Less is honored with a statue in a corresponding niche on the northeast. A cousin of Jesus, he became the bishop of Jerusalem at a time of persecution. His book represents the New Testament, which contains his letter to the early Church. Both statues stand upon white marble altars with pink marble panels and tabernacles closed by bronze doors with raised reliefs. These replicate the features of liturgical altars typical in the 1890s, when Masses were sometimes offered at side altars. Ionic features link both niches with the building's overall style.

Jesus' mother, Mary, and his closest followers, Mary of Magdala and the apostle John, mourn his death. This scene, just after Joseph of Arrimathea and Nicodemus have removed Jesus' body from the cross, was painted by Baron Pierre Narcisse Guérin and hangs in the west ambulatory. (Photo by John Glover)

A Venerable Instrument

The organ has occupied the north gallery for nearly two hundred years.
(Photo by John Glover)

T he venerable pipe organ in the north gallery will continue to serve the Basilica. At heart it is the historic instrument of exceptional quality built by Hilborne L. Roosevelt in 1884. This had replaced the original Thomas Hall organ (built 1819). Forty speaking stops control forty-five ranks, which comprise 2,427 pipes.

Repairs, cleaning and partial rebuilding (especially in 1989) extended the organ's service. In the current restoration it was retrofitted with twenty-first-century digital technology. With casters, the console is now mobile; it can be positioned for greater flexibility in the loft.

An elaborate mahogany case encloses the organ pipes. Carved laurel-leaf garlands and an egg-

and-dart cornice complement gilt-painted pipes on its surface. The two-story center section, remaining from the Thomas Hall organ, came from the hand of a highly skilled anonymous carver. New pipes added in 1884 required an extension of the case in the form of side sections.

The organ was the largest in the United States for many years.

The restored and upgraded organ console is lifted to its place in the north gallery. (Photo by William Bernard)

EXPLORING THE UNDERCROFT AND CRYPT

A A whole new life has opened up for the Basilica's undercroft. Accomplishing Carroll's and Latrobe's intentions—for the very first time—has been exciting for the restoration team. A graceful new double staircase descends to this lower level from the east ambulatory, behind the altar of reservation. It passes a door facing the archbishop's residence.

Eight of Baltimore's archbishops lie at rest in a mausoleum at the foot of the stairs. John Carroll's remains were moved here from a vault at St. Mary's Seminary in 1824. The others are Ambrose Maréchal, James Whitfield, Samuel Eccleston, Francis Kenrick and Martin Spalding on the south side and James Gibbons and Michael Curley on the north. The mausoleum was the only crypt area accessible to the public before the restoration.

The undercroft resembles a labyrinth of brick-vaulted chambers,

In the crypt mausoleum lie many of Baltimore's archbishops. [Photo by John Glover]

previously filled with sand and debris accumulated through the years. The floor-level has been lowered in certain sections, making more of the area accessible. Inverted arches of brick and stone bear the weight of the piers, which in turn carry the dome. New interior brickwork beautifies the undercroft and chapel areas. Foundation stones are visible along the walls. Workers

of bygone days have left their names in cement grafitti: July 12, 1863, Francis Gildea Bricklayer...David Gildea July 13, 1863...C. S. Smith A. Etheridge 28 Aug. 1961....

The new Chapel of Mary, Our Lady Seat of Wisdom, fulfills the cathedral's original plan. It offers an intimate place of prayer for individuals and for small groups.

The Chapel, graced by a statue of Our Lady Seat of Wisdom, is the gift of the Society of St. Sulpice. Sulpicians first came to Baltimore in 1791, seeking to carry out their mission of priestly formation, impossible in France during the French Revolution. To meet Bishop Carroll's need for native priests, they transferred faculty and the Sulpician seminary system. For over two centuries, Baltimore's Sulpicians have been forming American pastors. The domed bronze tabernacle, set with semiprecious stones, was used on the high altar from the 1940s until this restoration.

A statue of Christ the Man will greet visitors at the new west entrance. It was a familiar feature of the main level before the restoration. Busts of Popes Pius IX and Pius X recall the

The new undercroft chapel is dedicated to Mary under the title of Seat of Wisdom. (Photo by John Glover)

(Photo by John Glover)

link of the local Church with the Church universal. Pius IX declared the teaching of Mary's Immaculate Conception, as requested by the Seventh Provincial Council of Baltimore.

The Historic Trust plans future developments for the newly usable crypt, such as a "Hall of American Saints," a Basilica Museum under the sacristy, and a tribute to the men and women religious who have served in the Archdiocese.

The excavations have opened up more areas for storage, mechanical equipment and utilities and for two new restrooms.

TIME AND THE TOWERS

The two towers balance the Basilica's profile, their slender vertical lines complementing the massive curve of the dome. They serve the cathedral and civic communities.

Bell-tones ringing out from the south tower have marked the hours for Baltimore since 1831. A clapper rings the larger bell and two hammers strike it, producing different tones. A tracery of delicate grape vines wreathes its fourteen-foot perimeter. Two medallions on opposite sides picture the Crucifixion and the Madonna and Child. Naming church bells is a long custom. The inscription "Jesus-Maria" may have been intended to signal the great bell's name. The second bell is much smaller.

The south tower tells a story of time. Old and new combine in the clock.

In the crypt mausoleum lie many of Baltimore's archbishops. [Photo by John Glover]

Restoration work continued almost until the Basilica reopened.
(Photo by John Glover)

Satellites now control its precise movements and tell the bells to chime as the clock marks off the hours. Its hands and internal parts were fitted for a new operating mechanism. The new system is a far cry from the past, when the bells were rung by ropes pulled from below. The 1866 clockworks rang the bells, a great advance over ropes. However, the sexton still had to wind the clock vigorously for thirty-five to forty-five minutes each day. The process was electrified, and long-needed repairs completed, in 1986. With satellite controls, the hallowed rhythms now harmonize with the twenty-first century.

INFRASTRUCTURE IMPROVEMENTS

T Though visible features may take the Basilica back to the nineteenth century, the invisible improvements to its infrastructure bring it into the twenty-first. All its systems have been upgraded. Completely new heating, air-conditioning and ventilation required the restoration team to tear up the flooring and excavate sand from above the crypt arches to make space for ducts, which project architect Stephen Reilly calls a new "vascular system." Ducts lead to well over 100 air "diffusers" under the pews. The new system delivers cooled or heated air in greater force than before, with minimal sound.

Improved electrical systems allow historic fixtures to deliver the necessary levels of light. The building was completely rewired. New speakers address acoustical issues. Major improvements were made to the plumbing and security systems.

Compliance with the Americans with Disabilities Act, begun in 1994, now includes not only an entry ramp and restrooms to accommodate wheelchairs but also an elevator near the sacristy.

The newly accessible undercroft reveals Latrobe's reverse arches, supporting the columns above.
(Photo by John Glover)

CONCLUSION
FAITH AND FREEDOM INTO THE FUTURE

(Photo by William Bernard)

E Entering a third century of life, the Basilica of the Assumption of the Blessed Virgin Mary is poised for a continued mission of fostering faith and freedom. The venerable building recalls the past with renewed vigor.

The nation's first bishop and first professional architect had a vision, and that vision has been restored. For those who will pray here, for those who will visit, the message is fresh, a message as important today as it was in 1806. The building once more speaks of light: the light of faith and the light of religious freedom for all.

We Thank Our Basilica Benefactors

DONORS
(As of September 1, 2006)

Stewards of the Mother Church

Anonymous Donor
Mrs. Dorothy Williams Bunting★
Mr. and Mrs. Monroe J. Carell, Jr.
The France-Merrick Foundation
The Maryland Province of the Society of Jesus
Knights of Columbus, Supreme Council
Mr. and Mrs. Henry J. Knott, Sr.★
Dr. and Mrs. Rocco L. Martino
Mr. and Mrs. Arthur B. Modell
The Roberts Family
Mr. and Mrs. James G. Robinson
Mrs. Margaret V. Stine
The Society of St. Sulpice, Province of the
    United States

Benjamin Henry Latrobe Fellows

The Stephen and Renee Bisciotti Foundation
Mr. and Mrs. Paul J. Chiapparone
Mr. and Mrs. Peter Dwan
Mr. and Mrs. Jacques J. Moore, Sr.

James Cardinal Gibbons Fellows

Diocese of St. Petersburg
Mr. and Mrs. Michael J. Batza, Jr.
Bon Secours Health System, Inc.
Bon Secours Sisters USA
Ms. Mary Catherine Bunting
Mr. and Mrs. J. P. Blase Cooke
Donahue Family Foundation, Inc.
Mrs. Florence B. D'Urso
Mr. and Mrs. Stephen A. Geppi
The Getty Grant Program

Mr. and Mrs. Willard Hackerman
Josephite Fathers and Brothers
Mr. and Mrs. Carl T. Julio
Mr.★ and Mrs. W. Wallace Lanahan, Jr.
Henry H. Lewis Contractors LLC
The Linehan Family Foundation
St. Louis Catholic Church, Clarksville, MD
Mr. and Mrs. Alexander B. McMurtrie, Jr.
Mr. John A. McNeice, Jr.
The Ortenzio Family Foundation
Pallottine Fathers
Mr. and Mrs. Malvin A. Pavik
J. Bernard & Marie H. Rafferty
Redemptorist Fathers and Brothers
Mr. and Mrs. Brian C. Rogers
Mr. and Mrs. Michael J. Ruck, Sr.

Archbishop Ambrose Maréchal Fellows

Archdiocese of Atlanta
Archdiocese of Hartford
Archdiocese of Washington
Diocese of Brooklyn
Diocese of Orange
Diocese of Venice
Diocese of Wheeling-Charleston
Diocese of Wilmington
Anonymous Donor
Dr. Frances M. Baker
Mr. and Mrs. Richard O. Berndt
Mr. and Mrs. Carroll A. Bodie
Brothers of the Christian Schools
Connelly Foundation
Conventual Franciscan Friars, St. Anthony
    of Padua Province
Estate of Mr. Joseph F. Faimann

Mr. Brian P. Fimian
Miss. Lucy Ann Garvey, Esq.
Mr. and Mrs. Harold Honickman
Reverend Monsignor James V. Hobbs
Cardinal William H. Keeler
Knights of Columbus, Maryland State Council
Mr. and Mrs. Martin G. Knott
George W. McManus Foundation, Inc.
The Andrew M. Mona Foundation, Inc.
In Memory of Bruce Boyle Morrow,
    1956 - 1976
Dan Murphy Foundation
Raskob Foundation for Catholic Activities, Inc.
Mr. Charles Reeves
The Sheridan Foundation, Inc.
Mr. Jerry Stautberg
The Anne and John J. Walsh Foundation
Mrs. George Bernard Young

Archbishop James Whitfield Guild

Archdiocese of Cincinnati
Archdiocese of New Orleans
Diocese of Camden
Diocese of Fresno
Diocese of Harrisburg
Diocese of Madison
Diocese of Savannah
Diocese of Springfield
Diocese of Youngstown
The Amato Family, In Memory of Joseph
    Stephen Amato, Sr.
Ancient Order of Hibernians, Maryland State
    Board
Dr. Marie-Alberte Boursiquot
Caplan Family Foundation
The John Carroll Society

Mr. and Mrs. Michael Conway
Dr. John Quentin Feller
Ms. Bernadette M. Gietka
Good Neighbor Family Trust
Mr. and Mrs. Louis J. Grasmick
William H. Hannon Foundation
Hill and Company Realtors
In loving memory of Mary Ellen
    and Joseph J. Jaskot, Sr.
Mr. and Mrs. Francis X. Knott
Ladies Ancient Order of Hibernians,
    Maryland State Board
Mr. James T. Larkin
Most Reverend W. Francis Malooly
Mary's Fund Foundation, Inc.
Mr. and Mrs. Michael P. May
Mrs. Virginia McCaskey
Mr. J. Jerome Neser, II
Mr. Mark J. Potter
The Honorable and Mrs. William D. Quarles
Mrs. Margaret Knott Riehl
School Sisters of Notre Dame
Mrs. Patricia K. Smyth
Mr. and Mrs. Joseph A. Spadaro, Jr.
Miss Geraldine T. Tolker
Mr. and Mrs. Lincoln A. Warrell
Dr. Mary Devereux Weld
Mr. Wayne J. Zahner

ARCHBISHOP SAMUEL ECCLESTON CIRCLE

Archdiocese of Portland
Diocese of Columbus
Diocese of Dallas
Diocese of Lansing
Diocese of Portland
Diocese of Sioux Falls

Diocese of St. Augustine
The Aulbach Family Fund,
    In Memory of Mrs. Gertrude Aulbach
Dr. and Mrs. William F. Baker
Mr. and Mrs. Carroll A. Bodie
Mrs. Aurelia G. Bolton
Most Reverend William D. Borders
Anthony and Anna L. Carozza Foundation
Carrollton Bank
Congregation of the Sisters, Servants of the
    Immaculate Heart of Mary, Scranton, PA
Daughters of Charity, Emmitsburg Province
Mr. and Mrs. Hal Donofrio
Mr. and Mrs. George E. Doty
Dr. and Dr. James Ewing
Milton M. Frank and Thomas B. Sprague
    Foundation, Inc.
St. Gregory the Great Church, Baltimore, MD
Mr. Frederick W. Hill
Reverend Monsignor Robert J. Jaskot
Mr. and Mrs. B. Larry Jenkins
The J. M. Kaplan Fund
Mr. Michael J. Kennedy
Mr. and Mrs. Basilio Lachica
Ladies Ancient Order of Hibernians,
    National Board
Ms. Genevieve V. Manger
Mr. and Mrs. William McCallister
Mission Helpers of the Sacred Heart
Most Reverend William C. Newman
Ms. Mary Rhoads
Mr. Robert B. Rice
Most Reverend Mitchell T. Rozanski,
    In Honor of Cardinal Keeler's Jubilee
Executive Committee of the Mother Seton
House on Paca Street, Inc.
The Honorable R. Sargent Shriver

Mrs. Eunice Kennedy Shriver
Sisters of Mercy of the Americas
St. Veronica Catholic Church, Herndon, VA
Xaverian Brothers Generalate

PATRONS OF AMERICA'S FIRST CATHEDRAL

Archdiocese for the Military Services, USA
Byzantine Rite Diocese of Stamford
Diocese of Boise
Diocese of Cheyenne
Diocese of Gary
Diocese of Kalamazoo
Diocese of Kansas City - St. Joseph
Diocese of Lafayette
Diocese of New Ulm
Diocese of Rockford
Diocese of Salt Lake City
Diocese of Victoria
Diocese of Yakima
Adalman-Goodwin Foundation, Inc.
Aerosol Monitoring and Analysis, Inc.
Anonymous Donors (3)
Mr. and Mrs. Edward H. Arnold
Mr. Robert W. Barros
Monsignor A. Thomas Baumgartner
Mr. and Mrs. Ralph E. Bosch
Ms. Teresa V. Bosco
In Honor of Deacon Jean-Baptiste
    and Mrs. Alma Boursiquot
Mrs. Anne W. Breidenstein
Most Reverend Raymond L. Burke
Helen Marie Burns Living Trust
Carmelite Sisters of Baltimore
Ms. Lynn L. Carmody
Catholic Daughters of the Americas,
    Maryland State Court

Judge and Mrs. Martin E. Conway, Jr.,
      In Honor of Cardinal Keeler
Mr. and Mrs. Michael Conway,
      In Honor of Cardinal Keeler
Mrs. Susan S. Creitz
Dr. Sharon Dlhosh and Mr. William Bass
Dr.★ and Mrs. Edward A. Doehler
Most Reverend Timothy M. Dolan
Mr. and Mrs. Terrance Dorrington,
      In Honor of Cardinal Keeler
Mr. Michael Duff
Mr. and Mrs. Edward K. Dunn
C. Eby, Jr. and M. Eby Charitable Foundation
Mr. and Mrs. Francis M. Feeley
Reverend Martin E. Feild
Mr. and Mrs. Andrew J. Fenady, In Honor
      of Bishop Bennett and in Memory
      of Francis and Loretta Dolan
Mr. and Mrs. Thomas Fise
John M. FitzPatrick Family
Mr. LaMont William Flanagan, Esq.
Mr. Paul D. Flynn
Most Reverend John P. Foley
Mr. and Mrs. Stephen F. Fruin
Most Reverend Victor Galeone
Miss Lucy Ann Garvey, Esq., In Honor of
      Cardinal Keeler's Jubilee
Mr. and Mrs. Bill Ginivan,
      In Honor of Cardinal Keeler
Mr. and Mrs. George J. Gonce,
      In Honor of Cardinal Keeler's Jubilee
Mr. and Mrs. Alfred H. Graham,
      In Memory of Virginia Keeler
Mr. and Mrs. Alfred H. Graham,
      In Memory of Thomas L.
      and Margaret C. Keeler
Mr. and Mrs. Alfred H. Graham,

In Honor of Cardinal Keeler
Mr. W. Earl Griffin
Mr. James Hamilton
The Healey Family Foundation
Reverend Stephen E. Hook
Reverend Robert F. Hopkins
Hospital Sisters of the Third Order of St. Francis
Mr. and Mrs. Richard A. Hotaling
Mr. and Mrs. Terry L. Hurley
St. Ignatius, Hickory, MD, In Honor of Cardinal
      Keeler's Jubilee
The Irish Heritage Society
Mr. and Mrs. Stephen A. Kappes
Mr. and Mrs. Paul J. Kardos
Dr. Louis L. Keeler, Sr.,
      In Honor of Cardinal Keeler
The Keeler Foundation,
      In Honor of Cardinal Keeler
Mr. Brian M. Keelty
Mr. Sean P. Keller
Mr. and Mrs. Chul Hong Kim
Knights of Columbus, Fr. Wolfe Council,
      Abingdon, MD
Ms. Maryanne Knott
Owen and Erin Knott
Mr. Gary Kozel
Mr. and Mrs. Carl C. Landegger
Mr. and Reverend Steven Levy
Reverend Schelly Reid Levy
Reverend Paul Maillet
Mr. and Mrs. Ronald L. Mason, Sr.
Mr. Ronald L. Mason, Sr.
Ms. Anne Keeler McBride and Jack Manion,
      In Honor of Cardinal Keeler
Most Reverend John B. McCormack
Mr. and Mrs. Edward Monaghan,
      In Honor of Cardinal Keeler

Ms. Nora W. Moore
Mr. Matthew John Mosca
Mr. John D. Murnane, Esq.
National Council of Catholic Women
Most Reverend John C. Nienstedt
Oblate Sisters of Providence
Mr. John R. Page
Mr. and Mrs. Jeffrey C. Palkovitz
Monsignor Hugh J. Phillips★
Mr. and Mrs. Joseph H. Potter
Mrs. Bernice Raab,
      In Honor of Cardinal Keeler's Jubilee
RCM&D
The Rouse Company Foundation
Most Reverend Mitchell T. Rozanski, Christmas
      Gift In Honor of Cardinal Keeler
Reverend George W. Rutler,
      In Memory of Dorothy and Adolphe Rutler
Ms. Anna M. Schmidt
Mr. and Mrs. Daniel D. Schuster
Serra Club
Ms. Maria O. Shriver
Mr. Mark K. Shriver
Mr. Robert Sargent Shriver, III
Mr. Timothy P. Shriver
Sisters of St. Francis of Philadelphia
Susan R. and John W. Sullivan Foundation
T. Murray Toomey, Esq.★
Reverend Thomas R. Ulshafer, S.S.
Mr. and Mrs. Thomas Viola
Mr. Patrick J. Waide, Jr.
Mrs. Elaine J. Walsh
The Honorable and Mrs. Thomas Ward
Mr. and Mrs. Wilfred J. Weld
Ms. Mary Zepczyk
Sister Mary Thomas Zinkand, R.S.M.★